CONTENTS

Frederik VIII as King, painted by Otto Bache in 1909.

FOREWORD

Frederik VIII (1843–1912) and Queen Lovisa (1851–1926) were Denmark's royal couple for only six years, and their actions as King and Queen have paled in Danish historiography. The fear of war but also an economic upswing and social changes characterized their reign, during which the King and Queen worked to help the most vulnerable members of the Danish society.

I would like to thank the Royal Danish Order historiographer Professor Knud J. V. Jespersen, *dr.phil.,* who has been of great help with this publication. I would also like to thank the 15 June Foundation for providing financial support for the publication of this book.

Birgit Jenvold
Museum Curator

Frederik VIII and Queen Lovisa side by side, being received in Lemvig in 1908. The big tour of Jutland was a true triumphal procession for the elderly Royal Couple.

THE COUPLE WHO HAD TO WAIT

None of the Glücksburg royal couples has been overlooked to a greater extent than Frederik VIII and Queen Lovisa. As they are squeezed in between "Europe's father-in-law," Christian IX, and the "equestrian king," Christian X, a national icon, Frederik VIII takes up very little space in the history books, and his wife is almost never even mentioned. The events that transpired during the King's lifetime have paled with the passage of time, overshadowed by two world wars and Denmark's reunification with Southern Jutland. Frederik and Lovisa spent thirty-seven years as the successor couple, and "the eternal Crown Prince" waited in vain most of his life for a chance to play a more important role. When the time finally came, the couple were too old and old-fashioned, and the populace were already looking forward to seeing young Crown Prince Christian and his lovely wife Alexandrine take over. Frederik got six years on the throne before his sudden death in 1912, and rumours regarding the circumstances surrounding his death have survived when other aspects of his life have faded from memory.

Frederik VIII and Queen Lovisa awaiting guests at the Customs House in about 1907.

However, Frederik and Lovisa were more interesting than the history books suggest. Expectations of the young couple were great in 1869, when the pair were wedded in the Royal Chapel in Stockholm Palace. Specifically, the Danish Crown Prince and the Swedish-Norwegian princess were expected to enable Scandinavia to lay the conflicts of the past to rest and achieve symbolic unity. The couple could slide in and take over from the German-born Christian IX, who was unpopular at that time, and a Danish prince could once again become king. Frederik was

Pencil drawing executed by Frederik in 1860. The prince and his siblings were taught to draw by their father, who also performed morning gymnastics together with them.

everything his father was not. He was modern, well-read, and interested in changes to the political system. All hopes were in vain, however. Christian IX was on the throne for forty-three years and never made room for his eldest son. The successor couple fought for a place in the large international royal family, but they were constantly ignored and overshadowed. As an outsider, Lovisa was practically frozen out of her new husband's family, and she receded deep into private life and cared for the couple's eight children. Both the Crown Princess and the Crown Prince filled the long time of waiting with as many meaningful activities as possible, including charitable work, studies, and many hobbies—seldom have a successor couple been so well prepared for their future roles. The six years the couple finally got as King and Queen of Denmark were characterized by major domestic political conflicts that would be of importance in Denmark after Frederik's death, and each of them became involved in related events in one way or another.

The childhood and education of a prince

Christian Frederik Vilhelm Carl was born on June 3, 1843, as the eldest child of then Prince Christian (IX) of Glücksburg (1818–1906) and Princess Louise of Hesse-Kassel (1817–1898). His parents' marriage was harmonious despite their differences in personalities and abilities. He was very conservative and militaristic and did not wish to be contradicted. She lived up to the feminine ideal of the age: She was pretty, artistically talented, and intelligent but avoided overshadowing her husband. Frederik and his five siblings received an upbringing with an emphasis on duty, industriousness, and piety in their childhood home, the Yellow Palace in Amaliegade in Copenhagen. The family was not the focus of particular interest from the Danish populace in general, and its members lived quiet lives. Everything changed, however, with the Law Regarding the Order of Succession of 31 July 1853.

Kronprins Frederik. 1863.

A new young crown prince in 1863.

King Frederik VII (1808–1863) had been through two childless marriages to women of princely rank, and in 1850, he chose to enter into a morganatic marriage to Louise C. Rasmussen (1815–1874), who was elevated to the nobility when the king appointed her Countess Danner. The Danish king therefore had no heir to the Danish throne. A new future king of Denmark therefore needed to be found so that the European balance of power could be maintained. In 1853, the major European powers chose to recognize Prince Christian as the future King of Denmark. The ten-year-old Frederik was suddenly an heir to the Danish throne.

The boy's education was now focused on his future role. A particular innovation was that he was enrolled at an ordinary private school, Mariboes Realskole at

Frederik in uniform in about 1863. The prince dedicated himself to his military training with enthusiasm. He acquired a reputation for being a good comrade as well as a capable and dutiful officer. In his new surroundings, with his family at a distance, the young prince came into his own. Here, he acquired his lifelong habit of taking walks through the town to meet the populace.

Store Kongensgade 51 (now number 55), where he had an opportunity to meet children of upper-class commoners. However, the prince did not have an easy time of it at school. His classmates called him "the German prince" and isolated him. After two years, he was taught at home in a more traditional fashion.

Like all of the boys in the royal family, Frederik was also to be trained in the military. As a seventeen-year-old, he was appointed a second lieutenant à la suite. By 1863, he had undergone theoretical and practical military training with the Nineteenth Infantry Battalion in Nyborg and also spent a period with the Second Dragoon Regiment in Næstved. This was a happy time for him as it offered good comradeship and a chance to test his wings. Despite the protests of the Ministry of Defence, Frederik VII demanded that Frederik should have a full military education on an equal footing with everyone else. The King showed clear interest in the young prince and often expressed the wish that the prince should be given precedence over his father with regard to the succession to the Danish throne. In contrast to his parents, Frederik also had a good relationship with the very populistic Frederik VII and was also willing to spend time in the company of the king's wife, Countess Danner.

After he had finished his military training, Frederik was allowed to study at a university outside Denmark, something no Danish prince had ever previously had the opportunity to do. Oxford University was chosen, and he studied political science and history there. His time at Oxford would have a lasting influence on his political views, which became highly liberal and were characterized by parliamentary sympathies. Frederik's stay at the university would not be lengthy. On 15 November 1863, Frederik VII died suddenly at Glücksburg Palace. Frederik was suddenly Crown Prince and had to return as quickly as possible to a country on the brink of war.

The good Danish soldier

On 1 February 1864, Prussian and Austrian troops marched into Schleswig, and shortly thereafter, the Danish forces evacuated the old fortifications at the Danevirke. Patriotic feelings were running very high. Frederik wished to return to his old regiment, which was at the front, but Christian IX would have none of this. The risk of losing Denmark's crown prince was certainly great, but the prince's desire to participate was great as well, so in March, Frederik was attached to the army's Fourth Division under the command of Lieutenant General C. D. Hegermann-Lindencrone. This did not result in the direct involvement of the Crown Prince in combat. Rather, he participated in the retreat up through Jutland, the purpose of which was to spread out the enemy's troops and take a little of the pressure off Dybbøl. However, his participation and actions in the war were well received by the populace; the Crown Prince was considered to have acted as "a good Danish soldier." This contrasted sharply with the public perception of his father, who had been undeservedly hated for being too "German-friendly" ever since he had become king. This perception had a decisive influence on the Danes' view of the royal family after the war had ended in 1864 and Denmark had lost the duchies of Schleswig, Holstein, and Lauenburg. It was important to distance oneself from anything that seemed German.

Travelling in Europe

The tradition of sending young princes on a grand tour was still alive, and from March until June 1866, the Crown Prince was travelling with a small retinue; his journey took him to the courts of France, the Netherlands, Belgium, and England. A journey of this kind served several purposes. As the Danish crown prince, he was to represent his own country and present himself to heads of state. Also, the journey was intended to give him greater knowledge of the world. The Crown Prince acquired familiarity with art, culture, and new industries, and in England, he focused in particular on prisons and hospitals. Frederik did not spend every minute of this journey fulfilling various duties; however, there was time for a few brief amorous adventures in Paris.

For the twenty-three-year-old Crown Prince, the time had come to think of the continuation of the dynasty, and the grand tour was an opportunity for him to look around for a possible wife. In the Netherlands, Frederik was introduced to the wealthy twenty-four-year-old Princess Marie (1841–1910), and in England, he met his sister Alexandra's sister-in-law, Helene (1846–1923). The English princess and he were genuinely interested in each other, but Queen Victoria opposed a marriage of the two.

Travelling became an integral part of Frederik's life, and on several occasions, he functioned as a representative of his father. The Crown Prince represented the Danish royal family at the wedding of his sister, Princess Dagmar (1847-1928), to the heir to the Russian throne in Saint Petersburg in November 1866. Here—unlikely as this might have seemed—he made the friendly acquaintance of Crown Prince Frederick III of Prussia (1831–1888). The two young men had a number of things in common, including a highly liberal political attitude that contrasted with that of their conservative fathers. This new close connection, however, was controversial in the light of the war that had taken place only two years previously. The matter became politicized when Frederik received an official invitation to the court in Berlin. The situation was tense. Could a member of the Danish royal family accept an invitation from the country that so recently had thoroughly humiliated Denmark, a country with which negotiations were ongoing? The King was in doubt, but after a great deal of discussion, the government advised him to let his son accept the invitation. The Danish government may have hoped for a better relationship with Prussia, and that with the Crown Prince's help, it might be possible to recover some of the territory that had been lost. Frederik made a good impression in Berlin and received a friendly reception. He even got a chance to speak both with the Prussian king Wilhelm I (1797-1888) and—more importantly in the context of his mission—the head of the government, Otto von Bismarck. Nevertheless, there were no changes with regard to the question of Schleswig-Holstein, though the relationship between the two royal families did improve somewhat.

These early journeys strengthened Frederik's skills as a diplomat and helped him create good relationships with the royal houses of Europe, relationships that could be important in the future.

Sweden and Norway's "Sessan"

Lovisa Josephina Eugenia of Sweden-Norway was born at Stockholm Palace on 31 October 1851. She was the only surviving child of Charles XV of Sweden-Norway (1826–1872) and Queen Lovisa of the Neth-

Lovisa as an eight-year-old. In her childhood home, she was called "The Light Elf" and constituted the link between her parents.

Portrait of Lovisa, Sweden and Norway's "Sessan," painted by the Swede, Amalia Lindegren, in 1869. The portrait is in the Swedish national portrait collection at Gripsholm Palace.

erlands (1828-1871). All of the parents' attention was therefore focused on the little "Sessan" (shortened from the Swedish Prinsessan), as she was loving-ly called by her parents and, indeed, the entire population of Sweden-Norway. This nickname followed her for her whole life every time she was spoken of in Sweden or Norway. Her home was characterized by her parents' very differ-ent personalities and disharmonious marriage. Charles XV had a number of af-fairs that his wife tolerated without commenting on them. The King was lively, accommodating, informal, and greatly interested in art. Queen Lovisa had acquired a great deal of book-learning but was much more serious, reserved, and shy than her husband. She participated in representative functions as seldom as possible and enjoyed quiet gatherings. Nevertheless, she was highly regarded by the populace, not least because of her extensive charity work. A number of her parents' qualities would be reflected in Princess Lovisa, though in many respects, including as regards her appearance, she was particularly reminiscent of her mother. This was clear to everyone, and indeed, her father described her as "ugly but sweet." Her mother took charge of raising her and devoted every spare minute to her. Lovisa spent a very withdrawn and protected childhood in the company of her parents and carefully selected female playmates from the

Lovisa was raised by her mother to have a sense of social responsibility. She set aside part of her pocket money to purchase food, clothing, and other items for a poor child. The picture shows her in about 1867.

nobility, devoting much time to her studies. She was schooled at home, and her education emphasized both creativity and book-learning; there was a particular focus on music, history, Nordic literature, and foreign languages. Throughout her childhood and youth, it was impressed upon Princess Lovisa that she should be dutiful, undemanding, and generous to the poor. The princess's childhood, then, was very much influenced by her mother's deep religiosity. The princess was a lively girl and laughed often. As the apple of her parents' eyes, she was always the center of attention at home, but she was not exposed to large gatherings at home or in public.

Frederik painted in 1868, around the time he proposed to Lovisa.

Lovisa was never considered pretty, but her height made her an impressive figure. The picture shows her in about 1869.

The unification of Scandinavia

In the middle of the nineteenth century, the political and cultural idea of a united Scandinavia gained currency. Scandinavianism was supported by many prominent personalities, and many toasts were drunk to Scandinavian brotherhood. In a careless moment, Charles XV had even promised that Sweden-Norway would help Denmark if there should be a conflict over Schleswig-Holstein. However, the Swedish-Norwegian king had not secured his government's agreement with

this promise, and the Danes were therefore to be disappointed in their hopes that Swedish-Norwegian forces would hurry to support Denmark in 1864. The Scandinavian dream had shattered, but an engagement that spanned the Øresund might save a little of it. Charles XV had long been discussing the possibilities with regard to the potential marriage of his daughter to the Danish prince, Frederik, both with Frederik VII and, later, with Christian IX. None of the parties saw any real hindrance to a marriage other than possible reluctance on the part of the two young people. Frederik and Lovisa first met in 1862, and Lovisa later indicated that already then, when she was eleven years old, she wished to marry the heir to the Danish throne.

On 11 July 1868, Frederik travelled to Bäckaskog Palace in Sweden, where the Swedish royal family spent their summers. Already on 15 July, the two young people became engaged under the Engagement Lime Tree, a tradition associated with a particular lime tree in the palace park. The same day, the Crown Prince sent a telegram to Christian IX back home in Denmark, and the engagement was publicly announced. It is doubtful whether Frederik and Lovisa were actually in love with each other, but at least, they did not actively dislike each other.

"She might not be as pretty as your Olga, but she is smart, and she can turn the whole house upside down," the Crown Prince remarked to his brother, George I of Greece.

In July, Lovisa and her parents visited Bernstorff Palace in Gentofte, and the King and Queen of Denmark now had an opportunity to take a closer look at their future daughter-in-law. Christian IX remarked to his cabinet secretary, J. P. Trap, that Lovisa was not "finished" and that she behaved in a somewhat reserved and insecure manner. This does not seem particularly strange given her young age and considering the circumstances.

After she had become engaged, Lovisa was given extra schooling to prepare her for her future role as the Danish Crown Princess. She studied the Danish language and received instruction in the areas of literature, culture, and history. She could therefore write, read, and speak Danish fluently before she was married. She was also to become acquainted with the best-known Danish individuals in the areas of culture and politics, as she would soon meet these individuals. Enthusiasm regarding the engagement of the Danish Crown Prince and the Swedish-Norwegian princess was great on both sides of the Øresund. They were the young Scandina-

The reception of the newly wedded couple at the Customs House on August 10, 1869. From here, the Crown Princess and Crown Prince rode in a procession to Christiansborg Palace, where they emerged onto the balcony to be hailed by the people.

A small family gathering during the first dark years, in about 1871. From the left: Prince Julius of Glücksburg (Christian IX's brother), Crown Princess Lovisa, Crown Prince Frederik, Hereditary Princess Caroline (the daughter of Frederik VI and Queen Marie), Christian IX, Queen Olga of Greece, Queen Louise. In the front, sitting in the grass: George I of Greece and Princess Thyra.

Duchess Thyra,
Princess Alexandra,
Queen Louise, and
Empress Dagmar,
1892. Lovisa was
not received by her
in-laws in a very
friendly fashion. The
family, particularly
her mother-in-law
and her two sisters-
in-law, Princess
Alexandra of Wales
and Grand Duchess
Maria Feodorovna
(Dagmar) of Russia,
found that her
appearance and
behaviour left
much to be desired,
and Dagmar,
in particular,
disparaged and
isolated Lovisa
when she visited
Denmark.

vian hope. It also helped that Lovisa would inherit a very great fortune from her mother's family and owned a formidable collection of jewellery.

The wedding was a major event that lasted several days. First, inhabitants of and visitors to Stockholm had an opportunity to see Sessan's bridal outfit and presents if they could stand the long wait to get into the palace. On 28 July 1869, Frederik and Lovisa were married in the Royal Chapel in Stockholm Palace. An abundance of flowers and Scandinavian flags marked the occasion in the city, and ships in the harbour were decorated. Lucky individuals had secured tickets that let them watch the procession to the Royal Chapel. No effort was spared to celebrate Sessan's wedding in both Sweden and Norway. The mood among the Swedish-Norwegian populace was both melancholy and joyful, and there were folk festivities throughout both Sweden and Norway. The honeymoon was spent at Haga Palace outside Stockholm. On August 10, the long-awaited wedded couple arrived by ship in Copenhagen, where a six-day popular celebration had been prepared. The expectations of this new couple, and in particular of the realm's new crown princess, were great. The pair were both supposed to live up to everyone's hopes and find their way together, in their marriage, in new roles, and in a large family.

The Glücksburg Royal Family

The outer picture of the Glücksburg Royal Family is one of a warm and loving family that stood together and created impressive family relations among European princely and royal houses. It was not a pure idyll, however, and many of the tensions that did exist were focused on the Crown Prince and Crown Princess.

The relationship between the Crown Prince and Christian IX was never especially good. The King consciously restricted his son's influence and visibility both at home and in public. In contrast to his father, Frederik was a talented public speaker, but the King had made it a rule that his son would seldom be permitted to give speeches at formal dinners. Christian IX almost never gave Frederik responsibility for anything and generally did not like him to attract overly much public attention. Frederik felt a great deal of respect for his father despite the fact that they disagreed in many areas, particularly on politics. Despite being marginalized, he never contradicted his father. This ultimately caused the populace to develop a somewhat incorrect view of him. Some people believed that he shared his father's very

Frederik and Lovisa
with his sisters in
1870.

conservative views, others that he had no sympathy for the political dissatis-faction that spread in Denmark during the period from the 1880s until the turn of the century.

In many ways, Christian IX and Queen Louise's new daughter-in-law was not quite the match for their son they might have wanted. To be sure, she was rich and the populace were enthusiastic about the symbolism she represented, but privately, she left much to be desired. Her background irritated the Royal Couple. Charles XV reminded them much too much of Frederik VII, with whom they had never gotten along, and they were bitter because Sweden's king and government had not supported Denmark in 1864. Also, the Bernadottes did not represent a fine old line of kings; their royal house had been established only fifty years previously. If Lovisa's personality had been a better fit with the family, the other matters might have been forgotten, but in this area, too, there were problems. The straightforwardness and loud laughter that were characteristic of the Crown Princess did not fit in well with the habits of her in-laws, and for this reason, she eventually became subdued and sad. The liveliness to which Frederik had been attracted in the beginning was then suppressed by the deep religiosity with which Lovisa had also grown up. This did not improve the impression she made on the family—now she seemed boring and introverted. The Queen did not care for her habits and interests; most of all, the Queen found her daughter-in-law to be a petit bourgeois housewife. The somewhat difficult beginning of Lovisa's life in Denmark caused her to suffer terribly from homesickness, and this homesickness was worsened when her parents died relatively young. Queen Lovisa's sudden death in 1871 came as a great shock to everyone. Only a year later, Charles XV followed her to the grave.

However, Lovisa also found friends in the family, including the old dowager queen, Caroline Amalie (1796–1881), the widow of Christian VIII, and the youngest of the Crown Princess's sisters-in-law, Thyra (1853–1933).

The Eternal Crown Prince and Crown Princess

The Crown Prince and Crown Princess were popular—the Scandinavianist spirit ensured that. Rural Danes often had framed pictures of the successor couple in their homes instead of pictures of the King and Queen. Christian IX and Queen

Charlottenlund Palace was given to Frederik and Lovisa as a summer residence, and here they could be themselves. During 1880 and 1881, the palace was expanded with a dome and wings to create more space for the growing family.

Detail of the Stork Fountain on Amagertorv in Copenhagen.

The Crown Prince and Crown Princess in 1892 with six of their children: in the front Ingeborg, Thyra, Harald, and Christian; in the back, Louise and Carl. In the course of twenty years, Lovisa gave birth to eight children. The couple's large flock of children were a source of common joy. The Crown Princess took charge of raising the children, but Frederik greatly enjoyed playing with them, and it was to him they turned if their mother was angry with them. Before Frederik acceded to the throne, four of the children had already been married, and Frederik and Lovisa's second eldest son, Prince Carl (Haakon VII), had become King of Norway in 1905.

Louise suffered for a long time because of the perception among the populace that they were German-friendly, and the political unrest during the disputes over the constitution did not enhance the King's popularity. If the Crown Prince and Crown Princess had been more assertive during this period and exploited the situation, their legacy would probably have been different. Time worked against Frederik and Lovisa, however, and Christian IX's long reign meant that the situation changed. When the Royal Couple celebrated their golden wedding anniversary in 1892, a striking positive change of views in the populace could be noted.

Within the family, the successor couple kept to themselves for the most part. They had two residences at their disposal, one of which was Brockdorff's Palace

The Four Generations, painted by Lauritz Tuxen in 1902. Christian IX has been pompously staged as the founder of the Glücksburg dynasty. He is shown sitting on the throne of the absolute monarchs, holding a sceptre, and wearing an ermine cape. On the left stands Crown Prince Frederik (VIII) and on the right, Prince Christian (X). The little Prince Frederik (IX) stands with his great-grandfather's hand resting on his shoulder. After the painting had been unveiled, it was criticized for being out of step with the times. Frederik IX later disliked the painting himself, as the children's clothes of the period made him look like a little girl.

at Amalienborg (Frederik VIII's Palace), the other their summer residence, Charlottenlund Palace north of Copenhagen. Particularly the latter of these two residences became the preferred frame for their lives, and they spent as much time there as possible. Frederik and Lovisa had a common interest in language, literature, and history, but Lovisa's increasing religiosity contributed to dividing them. Their situation within the Royal Family and their long time of waiting as the successor couple might have brought them closer together, but they did not always understand how to support each other. They did share their lives with each other, however, and they undertook a number of journeys together, both within Denmark and abroad. And of all the Glücksburg royal couples, it is Frederik and Lovisa who had the most children.

On 28 July 1894, the Crown Prince and Crown Princess celebrated their silver wedding anniversary. This was a major event in which princely guests from Europe and Thailand participated. There was a festive mood everywhere in Copenhagen, and the streets were decorated with flowers and flags. In connection with the silver wedding anniversary, a new fountain was also inaugurated on Amagertorv in Copenhagen. Foreningen til Hovedstadens Forskønnelse ("the Association for the Beautification of the Capital City") had sponsored a competition to create a new fountain that could be revealed on the occasion of the silver wedding anniversary. The winning project, which was conceived by the painter Edvard Petersen and the sculptor Vilhelm Bissen, is the well-known Stork Fountain on Amagertorv in Copenhagen, which caused controversy in its time.

A long and busy time of waiting

Frederik started out with excellent prospects with regard to becoming popular among the Danes, but he ultimately lost their support. As Crown Prince, he was a member of the Council of State, but his father preferred that he not express opinions about anything. There were proposals regarding various posts for which he could have taken responsibility, but Christian IX did not wish to approve any of these plans. People were not used to needing to invent a job for a crown prince. And the government was not prepared to insist that he have a regular occupation.

It was difficult for Frederik to bear not having real responsibilities when so many people expressed the opinion that he should play a more prominent role. Howev-

The Danish military offered the Crown Prince an opportunity to show people what he could achieve. The picture shows him (in the middle at the top) with his brother-in-law, Edward VII of England, at the barracks of the Hussars in 1903.

er, he occupied himself during his years of waiting by taking on representative functions and by working with the various associations and institutions of which he was a patron. A contemporary description of the Crown Prince contains the following sentence: "With industriousness and interest, he strives to acquire insight into everything—factories, hospitals, the prison systems—all of the institutions that can enrich his experiences and increase his knowledge of the country and its people." He took a particular interest in conditions in Denmark's prisons. He frequently visited the prisons to speak with the prisoners about their situation and liked to try to effect small improvements of that situation. Again and again, he attempted to make conditions better for the prisoners, and his efforts irritated both the king and the government.

Frederik had very broad interests, and this is clearly indicated by his book collection, which is preserved in Her Majesty the Queen's Reference Library. Subjects such as history, literature, law, art, geography are well represented, as are travel memoirs. Another interest, perhaps one of a more popular nature, was the world of the theatre, which was one of his great passions. With great admiration and interest, he followed both well-established talents and the promising new actors of his day. He also enjoyed following all of the Copenhagen trends, including music halls and cabarets, and he was a well-known figure in the streets, where he often stopped to speak with people he chanced to meet. The Crown Prince also gained a reputation for being generous and benevolent, qualities he frequently manifested spontaneously on his walks.

A large part of the Crown Prince's long waiting period was spent on charitable work, and he took an interest in a broad range of organizations. A position that played a special role in his life was that of Grand Master of the Danish Order of Freemasons, a position he held from 1872 until his death. Charles XV, who was a Freemason himself, had encouraged him to join the order in 1870, and Frederik thus followed in the footsteps of a number of previous Danish kings. By becoming involved with institutions and associations, the Crown Prince obtained an opportunity to express himself in a context with regard to which Christian IX could not object. Frederik also received an honorary doctorate degree in law from Oxford University. This was a distinction of which he was very proud despite the fact that he characterized it as undeserved. In addition, he continued his military career, rose through the ranks, and made a good name for himself in the army.

One of his great interests was politics. He was a very frequent guest of the parliament, where he often sat and listened to the discussions. He had a strong interest in the political issues of the age and ensured that he was as well informed as possible. In contrast to many of the other members of the Royal Family, including his father, Frederik had had a subscription to the social liberal newspaper Politiken already when the newspaper's first issues were published around 1884. Though his opportunities to express himself were limited, he did find an outlet for some of his many opinions in the form of a series of letters to the editor of the conservative newspaper Berlingske Tidende. These were written

Frederik was often seen walking, either in the streets of Copenhagen or in the vicinity of his residences. During these walks among the populace, his generosity was often expressed very spontaneously in the form of cash aid to needy individuals.

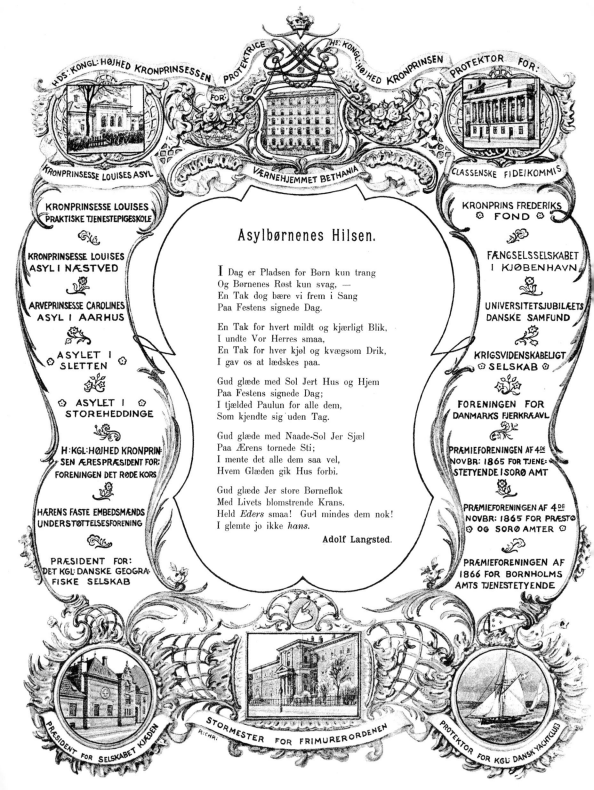

H.DS: KONGL: HØJHED KRONPRINSESSEN PROTEKTRICE FOR:
H.R: KONGL: HØJHED KRONPRINSEN PROTEKTOR FOR:

KRONPRINSESSE LOUISES ASYL

VÆRNEHJEMMET BETHANIA

CLASSENSKE FIDEIKOMMIS

KRONPRINSESSE LOUISES
PRAKTISKE TJENESTEPIGESKOLE

KRONPRINSESSE LOUISES
ASYL I NÆSTVED

ARVEPRINSESSE CAROLINES
ASYL I AARHUS

ASYLET I
SLETTEN

ASYLET I
STOREHEDDINGE

H: KGL: HØJHED KRONPRIN-
SEN ÆRESPRÆSIDENT FOR:
FORENINGEN DET RØDE KORS

HÆRENS FASTE EMBEDSMÆNDS
UNDERSTØTTELSESFORENING

PRÆSIDENT FOR:
DET KGL: DANSKE GEOGRA-
FISKE SELSKAB

KRONPRINS FREDERIKS
FOND

FÆNGSELSSELSKABET
I KJØBENHAVN

UNIVERSITETSJUBILÆETS
DANSKE SAMFUND

KRIGSVIDENSKABELIGT
SELSKAB

FORENINGEN FOR
DANMARKS FJERKRÆAVL

PRÆMIEFORENINGEN AF 4DE
NOVBR: 1865 FOR TJENE-
STETYENDE I SORØ AMT

PRÆMIEFORENINGEN AF 4DE
NOVBR: 1865 FOR PRÆSTØ
OG SORØ AMTER

PRÆMIEFORENINGEN AF
1866 FOR BORNHOLMS
AMTS TJENESTETYENDE

Asylbørnenes Hilsen.

I Dag er Pladsen for Børn kun trang
Og Børnenes Røst kun svag, —
En Tak dog bære vi frem i Sang
Paa Festens signede Dag.

En Tak for hvert mildt og kjærligt Blik,
I undte Vor Herres smaa,
En Tak for hver kjøl og kvægsom Drik,
I gav os at lædskes paa.

Gud glæde med Sol Jert Hus og Hjem
Paa Festens signede Dag;
I tjælded Paulun for alle dem,
Som kjendte sig uden Tag.

Gud glæde med Naade-Sol Jer Sjæl
Paa Ærens tornede Sti;
I mente det alle dem saa vel,
Hvem Glæden gik Hus forbi.

Gud glæde Jer store Børneflok
Med Livets blomstrende Krans.
Held *Eders* smaa! Gud mindes dem nok!
I glemte jo ikke *hans*.

Adolf Langsted.

PRÆSIDENT FOR SELSKABET KJÆDEN

R.CHR.

STORMESTER FOR FRIMURERORDENEN

PROTEKTOR FOR KGL: DANSK YACHTCLUB

under a pseudonym, but the author was easy to identify, as the newspaper always published the letters with the addition "From the pen of a highly regarded individual." He also exploited the opportunity offered by his silver wedding anniversary to make a political statement. Just that year, moderate politicians within the parties Venstre (the Liberal Party) and Højre (the Conservative Party) had concluded an agreement that had ended the nineteen-year regime that had been headed by President of the Council of Ministers (Prime Minister) J. B. S. Estrup. This had led to speculation regarding a new tendency in Danish politics. Frederik, who was a strong supporter of parliamentarianism, remarked in a speech of thanks he gave at the parliament that he hoped the recently concluded agreement would be "implemented with all its consequences." It should be the people's votes and not the King that determined who should make up the government.

The Crown Prince divided the opinions of the populace with his behaviour. Some saw him as refreshing, others as annoying. Many, particularly intellectuals, believed that his habit of moving around among the populace, speaking with people from all walks of life, and visiting prisons and hospitals indicated that he wished to be popular. Increasingly, the bourgeoisie considered his folksiness to be unworthy of a crown prince. Because he did not openly revolt against his father's conservative views no matter how much he disagreed with them, he also disappointed those who had expected to see him initiate significant changes to the monarchy. Frederik certainly had his faults, and President of the Council of Ministers J. C. Christensen remarked that he was much too easily influenced and too easily became enthusiastic about something, only to find it uninteresting a moment later. This created the impression that he was a somewhat fickle individual.

One of the innovations he implemented was the democratization of his weekly public audiences. Instead of inviting people in on the basis of their rank, the usual principle, he began having people summoned according to the order in which they had arrived. Suddenly, a high-ranking official would have to wait until the Crown Prince had finished speaking with and helping a poor peasant woman. This was a violation of etiquette that would have been unimaginable in the case of Christian IX, but Frederik retained the new system even after he had become King.

In connection with the Crown Prince and Crown Princess's silver wedding anniversary in 1894, this poem, whose frame features references to some of the couple's patronages, was published. While the list is not complete, it does give one a sense of the types of organizations and institutions in which the pair were particularly interested.

Idyllische Erindring om
Charlottenlund
31/7 95.

Lovisa's religiosity is exemplified by the Bible verses she painted for her children. Presumably, Lovisa wanted to give them some biblical words to take with them on their way out into the world. Today, only one of these illustrations of biblical passages is known to be extant. It was given to Lovisa's son, Harald, on the occasion of his confirmation and is today kept in the Royal Family's pew in the Church of Holmen.

Watercolour of Charlottenlund Palace painted by Lovisa in 1895. Lovisa was a talented amateur painter, and her great interest in art was recognized when she was made an extraordinary member of the Royal Danish Academy of Fine Arts in 1893.

An active and versatile Crown Princess

Lovisa's life was very much divided between her family and her charitable work. She embodied the feminine ideal of the age by remaining in the background. What the public did not see was that she was actually very active and had many

Lovisa with her firstborn child, Christian, the heir to the throne, in 1871. He remained her favourite, though she supported all her children throughout her life.

interests. Lovisa was quite intelligent and kept herself well informed with regard to what was going on around her. This applied to both domestic and international politics, and she followed parliamentary discussions closely. At dinners, she was always able to converse about the important topics of the age as well as matters that were of particular interest to her personally. She always made sure she was well informed about what was going on in Sweden and Norway and had ensured that she had obtained a good overview of the political discussions and transformations that were taking place there as well. She constantly made efforts to further her education by means of independent studies; for example, she learned New Testament Greek and Latin in order to be able to read the New Testament in the original version. Religion had been an important part of her life since she had been a child, and her faith became deeper and deeper with the passage of years. As her motto, she chose, "Omnia cum deo, nihil sine deo" ("All things with God, nothing without God"). Strong religiosity was very common during the age—including within the Royal Family. Lovisa was attracted by the Inner Mission movement, arranged Bible study meetings, and was frequently visited by Inner Mission priests, which resulted in some disharmony between the Crown Princess and the Crown Prince.

Like her husband, Lovisa carried out extensive charity work. The Crown Princess focused in particular on women and children, and an examination of the organizations she supported indicates that she was especially interested in "helping people help themselves." She was very active and liked to visit various institutions. Extant letters show that Lovisa became personally involved in minor matters related to the institutions of which she was a patron if she was directly asked for help.

Devoting herself to family life and her children was, however, what Lovisa viewed as her primary task. Already a year after her wedding, she gave birth to an heir to the throne, Christian (X). Over the course of the following twenty years, she gave birth to a further seven children in the following order: Carl (1872-1957), Louise (1875-1906), Harald (1876-1949), Ingeborg (1878-1958), Thyra (1880-1945), Gustav (1887-1944), and Dagmar (1890-1961). She sewed much of the children's clothing herself and took responsibility for raising the children. Even by the standards of the age, this was a large flock of children growing up, and via these children and the grandchildren, the family spread throughout Europe. In 1905, Frederik and Lovisa's son Carl was elected King of Norway as Haakon VII after Norway had left the personal union with Sweden. Their daughter, Ingeborg, married the

Frederik VIII greets members of the public from the balcony of Christian VII's Palace at Amalienborg on the occasion of his accession to the throne on 30 January 1906. As his motto, he chose, "The Lord is my helper." The proclamation was the first in Danish history to be filmed.

Swedish prince, Carl, and the ties to Lovisa's homeland were thus strengthened. All their lives, the Crown Prince and Crown Princess had a close relationship with their many children.

The long-awaited accession

The eighty-seven-year-old Christian IX died peacefully on 29 January 1906. After Frederik had spent forty-three years as Crown Prince, it was proclaimed from the balcony of Christian VII's Palace that Frederik VIII was King of Denmark. Finally, he had the responsibility he had so long wanted, and there was much to do. One of the most important political discussions of the time was about the Danish military defense, and this discussion was rooted in an old political conflict from the time of Christian IX. At the time of Frederik VIII's accession, the issue of Denmark's stance in a possible future war in Europe was the main point of conflict in the discussion. The threatening shadows of the war had long been sensed, but no one knew when it might in fact break out.

Queen Lovisa continued her charitable work and retained her role as patron of various organizations while also continuing to take charge of raising the children. Not all of the children were married, and the youngest, Dagmar, was only fifteen years old when her father acceded to the throne. Shortly after the accession, however, the family experienced great sorrow. The King and Queen's eldest daughter, Princess Louise of Schaumburg-Lippe, died of meningitis on 4 April 1906. Rumours to the effect that Louise had committed suicide due to a disharmonious marriage were widely discussed, and sorrow over the death of their daughter and constant gossip darkened the first year of the new king's reign considerably. Gossip and malicious claims had a significant impact on Frederik's and Lovisa's lives both during their time as the successor couple and during Frederik VIII's brief reign. Such gossip and malicious claims were transmitted via the press and in private conversations but also in anonymous letters expressing threats and accusations. The king undertook many journeys, both official and private, always together with his good friend, the chamberlain, Otto Bull. People gossiped about what the king and his friend might have been up to on these journeys, and there was talk about the King's extravagant lifestyle. There were many stories about various lady acquaintances for which no proof could ever be found. Even the king's generosity to the poor and needy offended some people. Nothing could be done to stop the gossip,

The official portrait of Frederik VIII, painted by Otto Bache in 1911. The King is standing on the balcony of his residential palace (Frederik VIII's Palace) at Amalienborg. An unusual feature of this painting, but one that is fitting for the King, is that it shows ordinary representatives of the populace to which he wished to feel closely connected.

and it would ultimately have a remarkably strong negative influence on Frederik's legacy.

Frederik VIII's reign

The years 1906-1912 were not characterized by major international political events that could have inscribed Frederik VIII's name in broad historiographic accounts. Rather, the period was characterized by social progress and by domestic political disputes. There were many new reforms during this period, and the King was very much involved with the extensive reform work intended to help the weakest individuals in the society. Aid funds and unemployment funds were established, and new laws were signed, mandating accident insurance for agricultural workers and help for mothers and children born out of wedlock. This period also saw the first steps toward women's suffrage: The King signed the law regarding the right of women to vote in municipal elections in 1908.

As the new king, he inherited a number of difficult matters from his father. One of these was the discussion regarding the status of Iceland in the Danish realm. As the Crown Prince Frederik had taken a strong interest in this question and in Iceland's culture and populace. He had even tried to learn Icelandic; Lovisa, too, had received instruction in the language. In the summer of 1906, in an attempt to get closer to a solution, the king invited the Icelandic parliament, Altinget, to visit Denmark. Already in the summer of 1907, the king, his son Harald, Danish ministers, and a number of members of the Danish parliament paid an official visit to Iceland in connection with which the group also made a stop on the Faroe Islands. This trip won Frederik the respect of a great many of the inhabitants of the Faroe Islands and Iceland. To the astonishment of many, he also chose to participate in festive cultural events. People therefore saw His Majesty energetically taking part in a traditional Faroese chain dance during his visit. During the North Atlantic journey, Frederik went to great lengths to speak with local people

Frederik on board the ship Birma on his way home from Iceland. The Danish members of parliament traveled on the ship Atlanta. At this time, it was not normal practice for a monarch to take official trips together with elected officials, and the Iceland trip is therefore an example of the King's democratic tendencies.

and attempt to understand their views and gain insight into the circumstances of their daily lives. To the King's great disappointment, no solution to the Icelandic problem was found during his reign.

One of the triumphs of Frederik VIII's reign was the major tour of Jutland the King and Queen undertook during the summer of 1908. The tour had been arranged by President of the Council of Ministers J. C. Christensen, who shared Frederik's opinion that the King should come into increasingly close contact with the populace. The tour was a way for Christensen to show the royal couple that there was still popular support for them, something the gossip in the capital city and the press often caused them to doubt. It was a great and encouraging success for them to be given such a hearty reception all the way through Jutland. A particular highlight, especially for J. C. Christensen himself, was his reception of the King and Queen in his home in Hee in West Jutland. It was unusual for a king to pay such a visit to one of his ministers.

The King and Queen on an official visit to France in 1907.

The Royal Couple and their retinue being shown around Askov Folk High School's garden on July 29, 1908. The tour of Jutland almost triggered a minor crisis as the company had originally planned to visit Skibelund Krat ("Skibelund Thicket") near Askov, from where one had a view of the lost land to the south. The outing was cancelled when it became known to the Danish government that the German Foreign Ministry objected to an official visit by the King to a place so near the border. The Germans were concerned about the possible reaction among pro-Danish individuals living in Schleswig. Nevertheless, the Royal Couple did visit the region.

During Frederik's brief reign, Denmark changed governments five times. This was a turbulent time! On September 8, 1908, the former Minister of Justice P. A. Alberti reported himself to the police for embezzlement of funds in the amount of approximately fifteen million kroner, which corresponds to about 968 million kroner in 2017 currency. The King found it necessary to demand that the President of the Council of Ministers resign, as Christensen had loaned Alberti 1.5 million kroner from the state coffers when he, Christensen, had been Minister of Finance. After this scandal, governments came and went in quick succession, and the defense issue ensured that politicians were constantly sharply divided. It was necessary to implement a reform that would establish Denmark's defence policy and present a plan for the future. The main subject of dispute was Denmark's relationship with the German empire. There was a political de-

Frederik and Lovisa with their daughter, Dagmar. The picture was probably taken in Nice on the couple's last trip together in the spring of 1912, shortly before Frederik's death.

The deceased Frederik VIII in a hotel room at the Hamburger Hof that happened to be empty after the King's death. One can only guess at the reason why the King was not returned to his own suite, but presumably, it was feared that the commotion would wake his family.

sire to remain neutral during a coming war, and this required a good relationship with the great European powers. Frederik's many years of diplomatic work and his relationships with the European princely houses contributed to securing potential neutrality. While Denmark's neighbours might have been reassured with regard to Denmark's position, there was still no solution to the domestic political disputes. Here, too, Frederik played a role, though in a rather unusual way.

When, in 1909, the new government was unable to implement a defense reform and lost its majority, it was difficult to say what should be done. No one in
Venstre wanted to form a new government, as there were deep divisions in the
party because of the matter. Frederik therefore made use of a very untraditional
political tool, one which actually conflicted with his parliamentarian views. He
suggested the establishment of a caretaker government. A government of this

On May 24,
Frederik's coffin was
transported through
Copenhagen to the
special train that
was to bring him
to Roskilde. From
here, the procession
continued to
Roskilde Cathedral,
where the King was
temporarily interred
in Frederik V's
chapel.

kind would be apolitical or at least not associated with particular parties, and the king hoped that it would therefore create the possibility of reaching agreement with regard to defence policy. The suggestion shocked the politicians in the various factions of Venstre and caused them to join together and form a new government, and in the course of the year, the matter was resolved.

Death in Hamburg

Even if one knows nothing of Frederik VIII, one may nevertheless have heard the story of the Danish king who died in a bordello but was surreptitiously brought back to his hotel to cover the matter up. This is a myth that has become a folk truth for the Danish population even though there is in fact, no evidence to support it.

When Frederik acceded to the throne, he was an elderly man, and his strength was declining just when he needed it most. From 1910 onward, the King's health only got worse, and in 1912, it all went wrong. In February, the King fell ill during one of his walks. His physicians established that he was suffering from a weak heart, and the King was confined to his sickbed for a very long time after his heart attack. It was not until the spring that he felt well enough to take a recreational trip to Southern Europe. In the company of Lovisa; the children Gustav, Thyra, and Dagmar; and a small retinue, he undertook a journey to the south of France. The King's health improved as a result of his stay there, and in May, the King and his retinue began the return journey to Denmark. In order for rendering the journey less strenuous and satisfy the King's curiosity regarding the new German locomotives, the company stopped in Hamburg on May 14 and took lodging in the Hotel Hamburger Hof. As usual, Frederik preferred to travel incognito; he used the title he had used most often in his youth, Count of Kronborg. At around half past nine, he spoke of taking a little walk in the mild evening air. This was his old habit, one he had recently denied himself because of his heart problem. There was later a great deal of uncertainty with regard to whether the King's retinue had known that the King had gone out and whether in that case they had neglected their duties by failing to stop the weakened King. No one knows where the King went, but already shortly after ten o'clock, a crowd of people had noticed that an elderly gentleman had felt unwell and had sat down on a stone step to recover. A policeman addressed him, asking who

The Dowager Queen with four of her children and four of her grandchildren outside Egelund Palace in 1918. Lovisa's children, Gustav (far left) and Thyra (third from the right), remained unmarried.

he was and whether he needed help, but Frederik provided only the name of his hotel. When an attempt was made to help him rise, he fainted, and a passing physician helped him get into a carriage and instructed the driver to take him to a hospital. When the carriage arrived at the hospital, the unknown man was found to be dead. The police report indicates that he died at about a quarter past ten and that the doctor on call had recorded as the cause of death that the elderly gentleman had suffered from atherosclerosis and had died of cardiac arrest. Other than a pocket handkerchief bearing a crowned F, there was nothing on the man's person by which he could have been identified. He was placed on a stretcher next to other unidentified corpses and assigned the number 1633.

At about two o'clock in the morning on 15 May, Frederik VIII's valet noticed that the King was not in his room. The court staff approached the hotel manager regarding the matter, whereupon the manager began making discreet inquiries and finally contacted the police. The manager was told that the police had received the corpse of an unknown gentleman at about half past ten. The hotel director went to the mortuary and insisted on being shown the unidentified corpse and immediately recognized the Count of Kronborg. Because the police refused to release the corpse before an autopsy had been carried out, the hotel manager was forced to reveal the identity of his special guest and argue that it was necessary to bring the corpse to the hotel. At the hotel, in order not to disturb the Queen, the King was laid in bed in a room that happened to be unused. At four o'clock in the morning, the deceased had been thus installed at the hotel, and the question was now how this unusual situation could best be handled. The hotel manager felt that one could pretend that the King had died in his bed of a heart attack, but because he had been seen in the streets and the police had completed a report, such a lie would have been quickly exposed. Early in the morning, Lovisa and the other family members were informed.

On 16 May, Frederik VIII was laid in a coffin, and a little memorial service was held at the hotel. By the coffin, Queen Lovisa held a brief funeral oration for her husband. Deeply moved by the situation, she unconsciously switched to Swedish, her mother tongue. The same afternoon, the Queen and her retinue returned to Denmark. On 17 May, the royal yacht Dannebrog arrived at Copenhagen with Frederik VIII's coffin. At the Customs House, the ship was met by family members, who boarded it in order to have a private moment. The King's sudden death had come as a great shock, and it caused great sorrow. The king's coffin was brought to Christiansborg Palace Church, where the king was to lie in a castrum doloris, that is, in a closed coffin. From the twentieth until the twenty-second of May, members of the public could come to say farewell to the deceased King. Christian X, who had just been proclaimed King, announced that the official national time of mourning would be "As short a period as possible. Those who grieve over Father's death do so without having been commanded to."

Of course, the German newspapers discussed the celebrity death, and many drew attention to the fact that there had been a forty-five-minute period during which no one had known where the Danish King was. While the area in which he had been walking was no more than a few hundred metres from his hotel, that area was a well-known amusement quarter in which there were music halls and also bordellos. Speculation ran rampant, and the Danish press soon picked up the theme. The former President of the Council of Ministers J. C. Christensen

Next spread: Amalienborg Sewing Circle's great contribution during the First World War made visible to the public the Dowager Queen's constant work for and commitment to the organizations of which she was a patron. This contribution caused the Danes to appreciate Lovisa even more.

Lovisa was laid in a marble sarcophagus in the Glücksburg Chapel, which had been finished in 1924 and in which she and Frederik VIII lie side by side.

even found it necessary to write a public letter in which he memorialized the king and attempted to shame those members of the bourgeoisie who had been willing to encourage malicious gossip.

Life as a dowager queen

At the age of sixty, Lovisa became a dowager queen. Basically, she continued performing the same tasks and leading the same existence as before. Lovisa had always been active and continued to be so during her widowhood. For example, she led a construction project, something that had not been seen in the Danish monarchy for many years. Already in 1911, she had bought the property Egelund near the lake Esrum Sø in North Zealand from the state at an auction.

She continued with the construction project during her widowhood, and in contrast to many of the Royal Family's other residences, Egelund Palace was Lovisa's private property. She used her new summer house regularly until her death in 1926. The palace was subsequently passed down to later generations of the Royal Family, but in 1954, it was sold.

Lovisa continued to pursue her various studies and interests alongside the extensive charitable work in which she still actively participated. The Red Cross was one of the organizations with which both Frederik VIII and Queen Lovisa had been actively interested and involved. In 1899, ladies' divisions of the Red Cross were established, the purpose of which was to collect money and sew various items that would be used in connection with the establishment and operation of field hospitals. The intention was that such hospitals could be used not only in times of war but also in cases of epidemics and other catastrophes. As the patron of these ladies' divisions, Lovisa carried out a part of the practical work herself. During the winter months, she led her own sewing circle at Amalienborg, which industriously provided linens and other materials to the storehouses of the Red Cross. She paid for all of the material herself. She made her greatest efforts on behalf of the Red Cross during the First World War. When the war broke out, she called together her sewing circle so that as much material as possible could be quickly produced. During the first five months of the war, Amalienborg Sewing Circle produced approximately three thousand items for a field hospital that could admit two hundred patients.

Many of the best-known items of jewellery used by female members of the Royal Family today were introduced to the Danish Royal House by Lovisa. The picture shows the Perlepoire Diadem, which is part of a set of jewellery including necklaces and earrings. This set is often used by Her Majesty Queen Margrethe II at gala events. Through the generations, the diadem has been worn only by Danish queens; it is part of the Danish Royal Property Trust established by Frederik and Lovisa in 1910.

During the last years of Lovisa's life, her health was poor. During the evening of 20 March 1926, surrounded by most of her children, the seventy-four-year-old Dowager Queen drew her last breath. The Dowager Queen's death in familiar surroundings and in the company of her family contrasts sharply with her husband's lonely end fourteen years earlier.

The legacy

The story of Frederik VIII and Queen Lovisa leaves one with a sense of terrible incompleteness. People had such unreasonably great expectations of them when they were married, and they never got a chance to meet these expectations regardless of how much they might have wanted to. While neither of them left a particularly distinct mark on Danish historiography, there are in fact still visible traces that remind us of this couple's lives and interests. Monuments and buildings associated with the pair are still standing both in Denmark and elsewhere. Also, some of the organizations and institutions they supported via patronages and by other means are still at work today.

Within the Danish monarchy, two remarkable innovations from their time survive. Frederik VIII and Queen Lovisa secured a lasting inheritance for the Royal Family by creating the Danish Royal Property Trust in 1910. This is a collection of items, including jewellery, that is passed down from monarch to monarch and can be added to but never reduced. In contrast to the Crown Jewels, then, items in the Royal Property Trustare not state property. Rather, these items are the property of the ruling monarch and may be borrowed by other members of the royal family.

Also, the Danes are brought together every year by a tradition that dates to the reign of Frederik VIII. The monarch's New Year speech to the populace has its origin in the toast to the fatherland that has long been expressed by kings at table on New Year's Day. It was Frederik VIII's idea that this toast should be expanded into an actual speech that would subsequently be printed by newspapers. In response to technological developments, this speech eventually developed into the televised New Year speech many Danes watch on 31 December year after year.

SUGGESTIONS FOR FURTHER READING

Aage Heinberg, *Frederik VIII og hans tid*, C. A. Reitzels Forlag 1962.
The only biography of Frederik VIII that has yet been written. This somewhat subjective biography is based in part on conversations with the king's second youngest daughter, Thyra.

Poul Duedahl and Peter Ramskov Andersen, *J. C. Christensen Dagbøger 1901– 1910*, Gyldendal 2006.
An interesting introduction to Danish politics during the decisive years following the System Change, seen through the eyes of one of the period's great political figures, J. C. Christensen. The diaries contain a number of personal remarks and impressions of Frederik VIII and Queen Lovisa.

Knud J. V. Jespersen, *Rytterkongen – Et Portræt af Christian X*, Gyldendal 2007.
The authoritative biography of Christian X, which, in contrast to earlier portraits, is based on the main character's own diaries.

Jes Fabricius Møller, *Dynastiet Glücksborg: En Danmarkshistorie*, Gads Forlag 2013.
Richly illustrated book about the Glücksburg dynasty and the role of the monarchy in Denmark since the nineteenth century. An essential book on the topic for all interested readers regardless of the level of their pre-existing knowledge.

C. H. Rørdam, *Svundne Dage, vol. IV, Hofliv hos Christian IX*, H. Hagerups Forlag 1918; C. H. Rørdam, *Svundne Dage, vol. VI, Mine referatsdage hos kong Christian IX*, H. Hagerups Forlag 1930.
C. H. Rørdam was Christian IX's adjutant from 1891 until the King's death, and his memoirs provide an alternative perspective on the Danish royal family during the reign of Christian IX.

kongernessamling.dk

Frederik VIII and Queen Lovisa
The Overlooked Royal Couple

Copyright © 2017
The Royal Danish Collection and Historika / Gads Forlag A/S

ISBN: 978-87-93229-83-9
First edition, first print run

Printed in Lithuania

Text: Birgitte Louise Peiter Rosenhegn
Edited by Jens Gunni Busck
Translated from Danish by Peter Sean Woltemade
Cover and graphic design Lene Nørgaard, Le Bureau
Printed by Clemenstrykkeriet, Lithuania

Illustrations:
Front page, p. 2, 4, 6, 8, 9, 10, 15, 16, 18, 20-21, 23, 24, 28, 29, 32, 33, 34, 36, 37, 38, 40-41, 44, 45, 46, 47, 48, 49, 50, 52, 56, 57 (photo: Iben kaufmann), 58 (photo: Peter Nørby): The Royal Danish Collection, p. 12: The Royal Court Photo Archive, Oslo, p. 14: Nationalmuseum Stockholm, p. 17, 54-55: The Royal Library, p. 26-27. Lukas Blazek/Dreamstime.com, p. 31 (photo: Thorkild Jensen): Christiansborg Palace, p. 43 (photo: Lennart Larsen). The Museum of National History, Frederiksborg Castle.